Fight Your

Medical Insurance

Nightmares!!

"Let Me Show You How"

By

Linda E. Meckler

Web site www.lindamecklerauthor.com

email lindamecklerauthor@yahoo.com

INFINITY
PUBLISHING

ISBN 978-0-7414-5589-5

Published by:

INFINITY PUBLISHING

INFINITY PUBLISHING
1094 New DeHaven Street, Suite 100
West Conshohocken, PA 19428-2713
Info@buybooksontheweb.com
www.buybooksontheweb.com
Toll-free (877) BUY BOOK
Local Phone (610) 941-9999
Fax (610) 941-9959

Printed in the United States of America

Published February 2013

From the Author

Linda Meckler

I have worked in numerous large, small, and hospital size billing offices for twenty-five plus years.

In part, I have written this book to educate consumers on optional ways to deal with insurance companies when disputes arise.

Obviously, you want your insurance to pay your medical bills. It's that simple. But! In reality, it's not that simple. If it were, I wouldn't have written this book and you would not be hearing the horror stories about medical insurance and how consumers' claims are not being paid, or paid unfairly.

In this book I cover a section on Medical Insurance, Terminology which will help you understand the language used in your Medical Insurance billings.

Medical Billing is very complicated and continues to become more so with each passing day. This is the way the medical insurance business holds on to their money, "Like Glue".

When you finish reading this book, hopefully you will have a better understanding of your medical insurance policy and claims.

Nobody can predict the future of health insurance and medical care in the years to come. But the information you will receive within the covers of this book will certainly be beneficial to you whatever the changes are.

Consider this book the start of a new knowledgeable relationship with your Medical Insurance Company.

Fight Your Medical Insurance Nightmares is for all consumers and is easy to read.

Disclaimer

I can not guarantee that your Medical Insurance Company will pay all of your medical bills, but I can share with you my many years of experience solving some of those problems. Good Luck and Enjoy!

Table of Contents

From the Author A

Testimonials and Reviews G

Chapter 1 1

Insurance Medical Terminology and Explanations in Alphabetical Order

Chapter 2 29

Medical Help for the Un-Insured

Chapter 3 35

Low Income Government Insurance Medi-cal or Medicaid, CMS, CHIP

Chapter 4 44

Medicare and Tricare

Chapter 5 58

Medical Computer Generated Information

Chapter 6 62

Important Phone Calls

Chapter 7 68

10+ Reasons for Denial

Chapter 8 82

Appealing Your Medical Bills

Chapter 9 88

Formatting an Appeal Letter

Chapter 10 106

How to Submit Your Medical Appeals

Chapter 11 112

The Collection Agency

Chapter 12 116

In Summary

Testimonials and Reviews

Linda Meckler wrote an Appeal Letter to my medical insurance company for me. The result was $26,000 was written off. I never had to pay a penny.

Mr. and Mrs. Foster
San Diego, CA

The medical insurance system is so complex and overwhelming that you feel powerless. I have been a Medical Provider and of course a consumer. In both these roles I would have benefitted from all the information included in this book. Armed with this book that is easy to read and understand and the format for actual letters that you can write, you gain the courage to change the things you can. The vocabulary is important to know and be able to use with the medical staff you will be confronting.

On a personal level, Linda single handedly got me through the maze required to get me set up with social security, Medicare parts A, B, and D, and secondary insurance plans when I became disabled. Her wealth of experience needed to be shared, and this book enables her to do that. We are lucky to have her on our side.

Dena Slonaker OTR/L, MSEd
Simi Valley, CA

Appealing your denied medical claim is a lot more successful when you know how to write to the insurance company! From 25 plus years of experience in the medical field, Linda Meckler shares what you ***must*** say. This book will get the results you want in most situations where an insurance company has wrongfully denied payment.

Shirley Ann Parker
Discoveries: A Journey Through Life
www.shirleyannparker.com

I just finished your book and it's great! I wish something like this had been written years ago! It's the way you put things in "people" language and not some jargon I can't understand! I especially appreciate the formats for writing letters. I never know how to even start! Thank you, thank you. I will take six books.

Carolyn Kloss
La Mesa, CA

When facing insurance company paperwork and what it means, you need Linda Meckler's helpful book. She provides personal testimonies to support what she is saying and guides you through the maze.

Even if you don't have medical insurance, you will face paperwork that requires a thorough understanding before you sign anything.

She covers that too. I recommend you have this handy book nearby.

John Wolf, author/educator
JohnWolfBooks.com Author of "Fantastic Tales"
http://johnwolfbooks.com, http://foxandquill.com,
http://generalspecifics.blogspot.com

As a retired professional educator of High School and College Level Teaching and having read Linda's book on Fight Your Medical Insurance Nightmares (let me show you how), I picked up a lot of good tips and information.

One of the main reasons of enjoying the book other then the context of information was the ease-ability of understanding the complexities of the insurance business. I recommend this book to everyone who deals with Medical Insurance Companies. They should definitely have a copy of this book and **read it**!

C. E. Ruzicka
San Diego, CA BS. ADM.
2 MA Degrees. Law, Finance, and Accounting.

For anyone having difficulties in getting your medical bills paid by your insurer, you should be able to find the answers in this book. It is clear and concise, has many examples of form letters that ask all the right questions, and space for you to insert all required information. This is a gem of a handbook to have at your disposal. and win your case!

Betty Lilienwald.
San Diego.

Chapter 1

Insurance Medical Terminology
and Explanations
in Alphabetical Order

In order to understand this book in its entirety you must take the time to read the Words and understand them.

Accept Assignment

- When a Medical Provider bills your medical insurance company, at the accepted, "**Pre–Set**" **contracted rate.**

- The patient then only pays for the co-pay, deductible or the percentage of your policy indicated on your Explanation of Benefits. This varies with different insurance companies. **Example**: Blue Cross, Medicare, Tricare, Etc.

- A check from the insurance company will go directly to the Medical Provider.

Account Auditing

This is when a person from your Medical Provider's Office goes into every open account (or balance owing) and asks the following:

- Was the claim billed?
- Was it billed to the correct insurance company?
- Was a payment made?
- Was an adjustment made?
- Was the secondary insurance billed and paid?
- Does it need to be re-billed?
- Does it need to be appealed?
- If everything is okay on the account, the account balance is now transferred to you, the patient to be paid.

Authorization (Approval)

- You need an Authorization before you receive any sort of surgery, x-ray, MRI or any other type of medical tests.
- This is received from your Primary Care Physician (PCP) or your medical insurance company.

- It will either be on a written form or with an oral authorization number for billing and tracking purposes.

- An authorization is important before any treatment or procedure is performed.

- If a procedure was suggested at the last minute, it must be authorized before the doctor continues.

- Without the authorization in advance your insurance can deny payment.

- You can always reschedule your appointment until after your procedure has been authorized.

Claim Form

- Contains your Personal Information.

- Your Medical Insurance Information.

- Can be mailed to your insurance company.

- Can get transmitted electronically.

Clearing House

- A medical claim form is submitted electronically to a clearing house then the clearing house electronically submits it to the appropriate insurance company.

- If a Medical Provider needs detailed proof of the "When" and "How" of the medical claim for a specific day of service, they can contact the clearinghouse and receive the documentation.

Consolidated Omnibus Budget Reconsolidation Act of 1985 (COBRA)

- The United States government created (**COBRA**).
- The Act stipulates that employer-based health insurance would remain in effect, should you be terminated or laid off from your job, provided that you paid the full monthly premium for it.
- This health insurance would remain in effect for a period of 18 months after your employment has been terminated, or sometimes longer under certain conditions.
- **http://insurance.lovetoknow.com/COBRA Insurance**

Contracted Rate

The contracted rate means the dollar amount of the adjustment the facility or doctor has been established with the patient's insurance company.

- Every Medical Provider has a contracted rate with individual insurance companies.

- This differs from one Medical Provider and insurance company to another.

- **Example**: You and your friend might have been seen by the same Medical Provider, for the same medical reason, but you have different medical insurance coverage. This is why your portion of the payment of the bill might be different than your friend's.

- Remember: The more your insurance company agrees to pay on your bill the less money you pay.

Co-pay

- The co-pay is the amount of money you contracted to pay with your medical insurance company.

- Each insurance company's policies are different.

- The co-pay is usually collected at the time of the doctor's, therapy visit, a procedure, as an outpatient, inpatient, or hospital visit, etc. The amount of the co-pay varies with each medical insurance plan.

- The co-pay can't be used to satisfy your deductible.

- A typical co-pay for a doctors visit can be a set amount or a percentage of your plan.

Current Procedural Terminology (CPT) Codes

- This is a code or number which is assigned to every procedure a doctor may perform. (surgical, diagnostic, etc) for billing and tracking purposes.

- It has a dollar amount.

- This (**CPT**) code is used by the insurance company to determine the amount of reimbursement that a Medical Provider will receive from the insurance company.

- Since the Medical Providers and the medical insurance companies all use the same **(CPT)** codes this ensures consistency.

- The medical fees that doctors and providers receive are different.

  Example: Doctor "A," performed a physical on a patient. The (**CPT**) code was (99396). The charge was $150.00. The insurance company paid $100.00.

  Doctor "B" performed the same physical on the same patient. The (**CPT**) code was (99396). The charge was $150.00 but the insurance company paid him $60.00.

- **The reason for this difference in reimbursement is:** The contracted rate the medical doctor or provider has with **each insurance company is different.**

- If your entire claim was not paid, there will not be a payment on the (**CPT**) code line.

- There may be a **Reference Number** telling you to read on the Explanation Of Benefits (**EOB**) which you receive from your insurance company about why a payment was not made.

Samples of CPT Codes:

(**CPT**) code **99214** Physical Exam **$150.00**

(**CPT**) code **90658** Flu Shot **$30.00**

Date of Service (DOS)

- This simply means the day you went to your Medical Provider for whatever reason.

- All the medical appeal letters are submitted by the **(DOS).**

- All medical billing payments are applied by the (**DOS**).

Deductible

- The deductible is the amount you pay before your insurance policy takes over.

- The deductible varies from insurance company to insurance company's plan.

Until the deductible is paid in full, your Medical Provider will not be paid by your insurance company.

- On your Explanation of Benefits (**EOB**) it will say what was paid to your deductible.

- Your insurance plan is on a calendar year, starting in January of that year and ending on December 31 of that same year.

Documentation

- These are your medical records.

- They can be from your doctor's office.

- Hospital

- Lab

- X-ray

- Etc.

- In order to receive your medical records you must fill out a Medical Release Form. This form will be provided by your Medical Provider or you can make your own (see chapter 9).

- Medical records are very important when submitting a medical appeal.
- Read them yourself to pick out any pertinent information needed that can help your appeal letter.

Eligibility

- This is extremely important.
- It means that you have been completely authorized to use the Medical Providers on your insurance plan.
- Your Medical Provider should call your insurance company before you even come into the office and make sure you are covered.
- You can even call your medical insurance or member services and verify that you are covered with the Medical Provider you will be using.
- For some reason eligibility can become very confusing.
- Never be afraid to make a phone call to your insurance company about your eligibility.

Explanation of Benefits (EOB)

- This is a detailed document you receive from your medical insurance company when they either pay, or don't pay your medical bill.

It will tell you:

- The Patient's name.
- The charges on the Date of Service (**DOS**).
- How much they paid.
- How much was adjusted.
- How much you now owe.
- It will give you an explanation as to why the claim was not paid.
- Possible Diagnosis.
- Bill Control Number.
- Claim Number.
- How to Appeal Information.
- Where to Appeal, address and phone number.

A Sample Explanation of Benefits Below:

Your Explanation of Benefits Form

Below is an example of an Explanation of Benefits form. If you have any questions about what these terms mean, click the link for further explanation.

Medical Explanation of Benefits

Direct Inquiries To:
Your Insurance Carrier
Insurance Carrier's Service Center
P.O. Box 123456
Hometown NE 12345-6789

For Questions Call:
Toll Free: 1-800-123-4567

Claim No: 05400566700
Group ID: G00079W8
Subscriber ID: 800858446
Subscriber Name: John A. Doe
Member Name: Jane B. Doe

Amount You Owe Provider: $25.00

Account No: 70053269ACB

Provider: John Smith, MD
Provider Group: Alegent Health

Reference No: 2004110110800472

Date: 02/16/2005
Page: 1

Please Review The Reverse Side Of This Form - You May Review Or Print This Statement Online Through Customer Access At chcne-m.com

Date(s) of Service	Service Type	Submitted Charge	*Negotiated Savings/ Write-Off	Note	Charges Non-Covered	Note(s)	Co-Pay	Deductible	Co-Insurance Amount %	Benefit Amount	**Patient Liability
01/18/05 01/18/05	Office Visit	200.00	50.00	PEX	0.00		10.00	0.00	0.00	140.00	10.00
01/18/05 01/18/05	Laboratory	50.00	25.00	PEX	0.00		0.00	0.00	0.00	25.00	0.00
01/18/05 01/18/05	Immunization	50.00	25.00	PEX	25.00	ZNA	0.00	0.00	0.00	0.00	25.00
CLAIM TOTALS		300.00	100.00		25.00		10.00	0.00	0.00	165.00	35.00

Other Carrier Allowed	Other Carrier Paid	Other Carrier Allowed minus Other Carrier Paid	Coordinated Benefit	Patient Liability after Coordination of Benefits
9999999.99	9999999.99	9999999.99	9999999.99	9999999.99

Provider: John Smith is being paid: 165.00

Subscriber: John A Doe is being paid: 0.00

Provider previously paid 0.00

Subscriber previously paid: 0.00

2005 deductible yet to be satisfied is if you use a participating provider and if you use a non-participating provider.
2005 Family deductible yet to be satisfied is if you use a participating provider and if you use a non-participating provider.

PEX The charge exceeds the allowable rate for this service
ZNA This service is specifically excluded by the plan. Please refer to the plan's General Exclusions

*Savings negotiated by your insurance carrier with your provider of service. The patient is not liable for this amount.

**PATIENT LIABILITY: Includes charges non-covered, co-payment, deductible and co-insurance amounts. Patient Liability may be reduced by Coordination of Benefits with a Primary Carrier.

Guarantor

- This is the person who is actually insured and can be different from the patient.

Health Insurance Portability and Accountability Act (HIPPA)

- The Health Insurance Portability and Accountability Act (**HIPAA**) of 1996 is the gatekeeper of the medical professionals to guard patient information.

- In 2003 the full version of (**HIPAA**) was enacted.

- Patients must sign a form with each individual Medical Provider, if they want their medical information transferred to other Medical Providers.

- The biggest threat in where your personal medical information will be viewed is when your Medical Provider submits your medical information to your medical insurance company for payment.

- If your medical insurance is through your employment, your employer also sees your medical information.

- Medical records are kept in private computer bases by many Medical Providers.

- Computers are the present and future for record keeping.
- This situation becomes alarming in keeping your personal information private.

Some States have set these limits for preserving Patient Confidentiality. They only give access to:

- Treating Medical Providers.
- Your Medical Insurance Company.
- Third party Mental Health Providers.
- Research Providers.
- Families of the consumer.
- Law Enforcement Agencies under certain conditions. (see patient confidentiality)

Health Maintenance Organization (HMO)

Description:

- An (**HMO**) is the least expensive medical plan available.
- This plan is available from many insurance plans.

- It is not always the most efficient.

- A doctor may be denied the request for the best treatment for, you, the patient.

- Many insurance companies offer different plans for your choice. It is up to you to pick the right one that fits you and your family needs and budget.

- Primary Care Physician (**PCP**) who manages your entire healthcare needs.

- Low co-pays

- You need a referral from your Primary Care Physician (**PCP**) to see a specialist.

- This will either be on paper or oral referral numbers. This is received directly from your (**PCP**) office or your medical insurance company. **Example**: Kaiser Permanente, Blue Cross, Blue Shield, Aetna, HealthNet, Medicare and others that may offer (**HMOs)** in your area.

- Call your insurance carrier for information on (**HMOs**) for specific requirements.

International Classification of Diseases, Ninth Revision

(ICD-9) Code or (ICD) Code

- An (**ICD**) code, number, is a list containing diseases for surgical, therapeutic, and diagnostic procedures.
- It is used by all Medical Providers and medical insurance companies for billing and tracking purposes.
- This is why you went to your Medical Provider in the first place.
- **Example:** An Ear Infection. Insurance companies assign that ear infection an (**ICD**) code number.

The CPT Codes (reason for doctor's visit with dollar amount) and ICD Codes (diagnosis) are computer codes. This is how the insurance companies pay the Medical Providers. (ref. above)

Identification Number (ID#)

- This is the number printed on **your** medical Insurance Identification card. (**ID#**)
- In the past it was your Social Security Number.

- Today, because of **Identity Theft** concerns, the (**ID#**) is now a number your medical insurance company has chosen to keep your private information, even more private.

Itemized Bill

- This is a bill you receive from your Medical Provider usually in the mail. It has on it:

    1. The Patient's name.
    2. Date of service (**DOS).**
    3. The name of the Medical Provider
    4. The address of the Medical Provider (**POS**).
    5. Your medical visit is broken down line by line with a dollar amount.

Example:	Office Visit	$75.00
	Lab	$50.00
	X-ray	$50.00
Total		$175.00

Medical Provider

- Doctor's visit
- Laboratory

- X-ray
- Hospital
- Ambulance transport
- Therapist
- Etc.

Non-Participating Provider

- This is a Medical Provider who does not have a contract with your insurance company.
- In many cases, this pertains to a (**PPO**). You will be paying more for your medical bill.
- Always ask when seeing a new Medical Provider if they are contracted with your insurance company.

Out-of-Network

- Preferred Provider Organization (**PPO**) It has a list of providers that it uses in their "network"
- They are maintained by contract with your Medical Provider and your Medical Insurance.
- If the provider is **Not** in your contractual agreement then they are considered out-of-network and you will pay more for your bill than if you stayed within your contract.

- If you choose **(PPO)** you pay a little more in premiums but you can go out of net-work and use doctors of your choice.

- The **(PPO)** structure will pick up portions of the bill but the payment to the Medical Provider will **Not** be as high if as if they were within the network.

Participating Provider

- This is a Medical Provider who is contracted with your Medical Insurance. Example: Doctor, Hospital, Therapist, etc.

- Payments will be applied to your medical bill based upon your medical insurance policy.

Patient Confidentiality

- A letter signed by the consumer, on file in the provider's office, saying who can get the information will open the door for (a specific family member or friend) to speak on your behalf about your medical care and bills or have a signed Power of Attorney.

- The provider's office is **not allowed** to give out any information about you to another person except a spouse for **billing purposes only**. This may need a signed authorization form.

- However, if you call your provider's office and want to discuss your **spouse's medical problem, a signed authorization form is needed.**

- Parents may only inquire about their children's medical condition and medical bills, if they are less than eighteen years of age.

- Eighteen years old and over are considered an adult.

Phone Log

- This is a log, report, or documentation which you do with each phone call to your Medical Provider's office and your medical insurance company.

It should have the following information:

- The name of the Medical Provider you are calling.

- The name of the person you spoke with.

- The date you called.

- The date of service you called about.

- The reason for your call.

- The outcome of your call.

- You can use this log or documentation if and when you need to appeal your medical bill.

Above all no matter what system you use keep detailed records of all communications with your Medical Provider and Insurance Company.

Place of Service (POS)

- This is where your medical services were provided such as:

    1. Doctor's office visit.
    2. Private Laboratory visit.
    3. X-ray visit.
    4. Etc.

Preferred Provider Organization (PPO)

Description:

- It is less Restrictive than an (**HMO**).
- You can choose your own doctor.
- You can visit a specialist without a referral for any medical problem.

- If you choose a doctor who is not in your **PPO** network your medical bill will be higher.
- If you stay within your network your insurance will be paid at a higher rate.
- Call your local insurance carrier for their specific (**PPO**) requirements.

Pre-existing Condition

- A condition the insurance company can use to deny you insurance when applying to their company for coverage.
- They use it when the person applying for medical insurance has been diagnosed and treated previously for an illness that is ongoing.
- If you are employed, the pre-existing condition will be excluded for 12 months (18 months if you are a late enrollee).
- It applies to conditions in the six months leading up to enrollment.
- Each state is different. Always keep this in mind when you are changing employment and locations.

Private Insurance

Description:

- There are a vast number of private insurance companies to choose from.
- You can be connected with private insurance through your employer's group plan.
- You can also purchase an "individual" plan on your own that is right for you and your family.
- Choose whatever is best for you out of the plans available. **Example:** Blue Cross.
- Private insurance gives you much more freedom.
- You can pick the doctor.
- You can see a specialist without a referral.
- You do not need to stick with a certain list of doctors on any particular plan.
- The cost of private insurance is higher than an Advantage Plan, (**HMO)** or (**PPO)**. These plans are discussed in detail in the section under Medicare. (**Chapter 4**)

Referral

- You need a referral from your Primary Care Physician (**PCP**) before you can see a specialist. This applies especially with **(HMO)** Insurance.
- This will either be in writing or orally set up between the doctor, insurance and patient.

Retro Authorization

- A Retro Authorization is needed when a procedure was performed without the doctor's office obtaining a prior authorization.
- The doctor's office is responsible for obtaining a Retro Authorization for the procedure that has already been performed.
- Sometimes, this is possible and sometimes, the insurance company will absolutely deny this request.
- Then the patient is responsible for a procedure that was performed without authorization.

Secondary Medical Insurance

- If you have another insurance in addition to the primary insurance, the secondary insurance can be billed in different ways:

  Example 1: Let us use **Medicare** as the primary insurance and **AARP** as the secondary insurance. **Medicare** can be billed electronically as a crossover. Meaning, when Medicare pays the computer will automatically electronically send the information to **AARP**. Then **AARP** will pay on this date of service.

Example 2: It can also be paid by paper claim. This takes much more work for the Medical Provider's office. When the Explanation of Benefits (**EOB**) arrives in their office and the Date of Service (**DOS**) is paid, a copy of the (**EOB**) is then mailed to **AARP** with a claim form. This takes a longer time to get a payment from **AARP**.

Example 3: Other insurance companies other than Medicare and **AARP**, which have secondary insurance, can go electronically, as described above or billed by a paper claim.

- **Some Medical Provider's offices do not bill the secondary insurance company, therefore, you, the patient, are responsible to bill your own secondary insurance company.**
- Be aware of this when you become a new patient.
- Then it is up to you the patient to make a copy of your (**EOB**) with the payment or non-payment on it and mail it to your secondary insurance company.

State Disability Insurance (SDI)

Requirements:

- Illness medical or mental, injury, disability, or pregnancy which prevents you from working your regular job.
- When you are not injured on the job.
- When you are injured on the job that would be Workmen's Compensation Insurance.
- A form is filled out by your Medical Provider and you.
- It lasts from 39 to 52 weeks.
- If you return to work part time you can receive (**SDI**) for longer than 52 weeks.
- There isn't any immigration or proof of citizenship required.
- In California these people are not covered by (**SDI**).

  a) Some Domestic Workers

  b) Most Government Employees

  c) Interstate Railroad Workers

  d) Claim a Religious Exemption

  e) Some Non-profit Employees.

- There are 4 states which provide State Disability: Each state or Commonwealth handles their own state.

    a) California

    b) Hawaii

    c) New Jersey

    d) New York

    e) The Commonwealth Of Puerto Rico

- Check the website under state disabilities for complete information regarding (**SDI).**

Super Bill

- A form the Medical Provider's office uses for each patients visit. It includes:
- Patient's Name.
- Date of Service (**DOS**).
- Place of Service (**POS**).
- (**CPT)** code(s) (This is the reason for the visit with a dollar amount).
- **(ICD)** code (diagnosis)
- **Note:** With this form you can bill your own medical insurance.

Timely Filing

- Timely Filing has to do with filing late. This means from the Date of Service (**DOS**) of your medical visit, the clock starts ticking.

- Your claim form must be received in your medical, insurance, company office by a certain date provided by the insurance company. If it is not, the Medical Provider must provide proof that it was sent.

Worker's Compensation

Description:

- Worker's Compensation Insurance started in Wyoming in 1911.

- This is medical insurance provided to you from your employer.

- This insurance mainly is to protect you, if you are hurt on the job.

- You must report the incident to your supervisor.

- Fill out the proper forms.

- Then start receiving medical care immediately.

- It might be wise to find a competent workmen's compensation attorney early in the treatment plan.

- Check out the worker's compensation websites for more detailed information.

All the care that is prescribed by your doctor is reviewed by a panel which must approve the treatments regardless of what your doctor or therapists think is necessary. This can become complicated and frustrating for your Medical Provider and, you, the patient.

Chapter 2

Medical Help for the Un-Insured

---

211 Phone Number or www.211.org

Examples:

- Lost Your Job?
- Can't Afford Medical Coverage?
- Your Employer Doesn't Provide Medical Coverage?
- Part Time Worker?
- Disabled Can't Work?
- Where can I go to get help for my child?
- Are there any free clinics available?
- These people have all this information and more at their fingertips.
- The 211 phone number may not be in your area. In that case you can call your information operator at 411.

- You can also use your local telephone book under, city, county state agencies for help information.

If you need to know what is available for you or your children, the first thing you should do is call 211. This is the new information line for all city and county help programs. Volunteers man the phones 24 hours a day.

Discount Cards

- Discount cards are not a medical insurance plan.
- You pay a monthly fee.
- You receive a cash discount on medical/ pharmacy.
- You pay for medical care at the time of your visit.
- The care you can receive with the Discount Card is usually just for minor doctor visits and if your medical care becomes more complicated your card may not help you, especially; if you are not covered by a regular medical plan.
- Discount cards will provide you with access to a large list of Medical Providers which may or may not be updated.

- Be wary of hidden administration fees. Such as: Paying a fee when writing a check, or credit card charges.

- If you are unhappy with your discount card, you can contact the Better Business Bureau or your State Insurance Department Bureau.

- Some Discount Card Plans are not worth the time or effort, so be careful when choosing a plan for yourself.

Urgent Care

- Urgent Care Facilities are medical facilities that take care of minor problems.

- With a complex problem, they are usually taken by ambulance to a hospital emergency room, or the person has the option to arrive at a hospital emergency room by car.

- **The ambulance transport is very expensive and insurance companies are very picky and will refuse payment if they feel the patient could have arrived at the emergency room by their own means of transportation.**

- If you have a minor ailment, urgent care is the facility to utilize.

- They charge a minimal fee.

- You do not have to wait for hours.

- This is a great way to receive medical care at a lower fee when you lack medical insurance coverage.

Free Clinics

- Free Clinics are usually county clinics that work on a sliding scale by income.

- You need to find out the highest amount they will charge you, before you make your appointment. The lower your income is, the less money you will be required to pay, if any at all.

- If your medical problem is greater than a fast trip to the doctor for a prescription, you will have to pay more for the service. You can find this information at websites under "free medical care" or "free clinics" for your city and state.

- This information is also listed in your telephone book under city and county sections.

Private Doctor's Offices

- Even when you don't have medical insurance, you can still make an appointment and visit a private doctor.

- You have the option of asking for a cash discount, since you do not have medical insurance.

- You will probably have to pay for your doctor's visit on that day of your visit, unless other arrangements have been made in advance.

Problem When Un-insured

- If you need laboratory work, x-ray, MRI, or surgery, this is where the cost of your medical care becomes sky-high.

- When you don't have medical insurance or a fat wallet, your doctor may not be able to give you the medical care you need.

- This is also the reason some doctors will not take patients when they do not have medical insurance.

Emergency Rooms

- Thousands of people now flock to the hospital emergency rooms for everyday medical care. This is the only medical facility available, without paying for their medical care at the time of the visit. People are willing to wait long hours, clogging the flow of real trauma cases.

- Some emergency rooms are well aware of this situation. They realize people are using the emergency room doctors as their own family doctor. They now triage (group) their patient's medical complaints.

- The trauma cases are put in beds immediately. Trauma cases are life and death situations.

- Minor medical problems are seen by other medical staff for a set fee. The emergency room tries very hard to collect this fee while the patient is right there in the emergency room.

- What happens with emergency room patient's visit? The patient is seen by the doctor. Next, he or she receives the proper treatment and, if necessary, a prescription is provided. The patient has been taken care of, leaves the facility, and may never be heard of again.

- **Result**, The medical facility or the doctors, in most cases, never receive payment for the services provided. Many emergency rooms have shut their doors due to lack of funds to support the needy.

There is an inherent conflict within the profession of medicine. Doctors' and all medical professionals' want to make a living but at the same time want to help people. They are as frustrated as you are.

Chapter 3

Low Income Government Insurance

Medi-cal or Medicaid, CMS, CHIP

- **Here is a list of government assisted programs in California that low income families can take advantage of.**
- **If you do not live in California there will be programs provided by your state.**

Medi-cal/Adults (1-800-541-5555)

Requirements:

- There are tight restrictions on receiving Medi-Cal: In other states other than California it is called, Medicaid. Either one is a Public Insurance Health - Care, Program, which provides health care services for low-income individuals and families. But they must meet specific eligibility requirements, such as any of the following:
- A single parent with minor children.

- Are on Social Security Disability.
- Are unemployed.
- Pregnant women.
- Have low income.

Non-Covered Drugs:

- When you go to the pharmacy to have a prescription filled and the pharmacist says, medi-cal doesn't cover this brand. you have several options:
- Ask the pharmacist which brand name is covered under medi-cal.
- He should know because this information is in the computer program.
- Ask the pharmacist to call the doctor's office to get authorization to replace your prescription request?
- You may have to physically return to your doctor's office to request a new written prescription.

Treatment Authorization Request (TAR)

- If all the above options fail then the pharmacist will, at your request, submit a Treatment Authorization Request (**TAR**) and submit it to the

(**TAR**) office for approval and in this way you may receive your medication.

- If your appeal is denied then you have 180 days from the (**TAR**) decision date or action date or denial date to send an appeal.

Send the Appeal to:

Medi-cal Operations Division Headquarters

Tar Administrative Remedy Section

1501 Capitol Avenue, Suite 71-3002

MS 4505, P.O. Box 997419,

Sacramento, CA 95899-7419

Submit With Appeal:

- A copy of the original denied or modified **(TAR)**.
- Dates of Service in dispute.
- The reason the **(TAR)** should be granted.
- Any additional documentation including Medical Records.
- A new (**TAR**)

1-800-541-5555

http://www.dhcs.ca.gov/provgovpart/Pages/Billing.aspx

To follow and throughout the remainder of the book I will submit different examples of my Personal and Professional experiences on how the Insurance "Business World" works. Example # 1

Working at Rebilling Medi-cal

Back in the early 90's I was working in an office with two physicians. One of my various jobs was to re-bill Medi-Cal for improper surgery billings for outpatient, surgery. Some of the claims were never billed or never billed correctly. This had been going on for almost two years. Evidently, the person who had this job before me was not knowledgeable in how Medi-Cal worked or was unable to manage the overwhelming task.

In Medi-Cal billing there is a time limit, starting from the Date of Service (**DOS**) to when it is mailed out and received by Medi-Cal. One of the many reasons a Medical Provider does not want a Medi-Cal patient is because of the large amount of paperwork involved in getting paid.

If they have a billing person working on their Medi-Cal accounts who does not have the knowledge to bill these claims correctly, they will never receive a penny of their well deserved fee.

My job was to type up stacks and stacks of overdue outpatient surgery claims, each one representing a patient and their specific surgery. (An outpatient surgery is when a patient is in the hospital for less than 24 hours.)

This was thousands upon thousands of dollars the doctor had never received in payment, and may never receive.

When I said type, I mean type on a typewriter! Even though we had a computer, in fact several computers for our insurance billing use, in order to bill Medi-Cal for these overdue outpatient claims, they had to be typed on a specific form (appeal form), in a specific way, and then be submitted to Medi-Cal in a specially printed envelope, provided by Medi-Cal.

The patient never receives a bill because he or she is on Medi-Cal and never knows their doctor did not get paid for their services.

Several months later I was called into the office of one of the doctors. I immediately thought, "Oh, now what have I done?" He took me out to where all the other staff members were gathered, about ten people in all, shook my hand, and said, "I haven't received a check from Medi-Cal for over a year on my outpatient surgery patients. This month I received two and they were both in the thousands of dollars. Thank you." Everybody clapped. I did not receive any money, but I still feel special when I think about this incident. When the billing is done right the medical provider will usually see Medi-cal patients.

Medi-cal for Children

There are many medi-cal programs for children depending on their specific needs. The most popular plan is:

Healthy Families Plan

Requirements:

- Ages 0 – 18.
- No medical Insurance from an Employer Health Plan involving their parents within the last three months.
- Must live in California.
- Children who aren't enrolled in Medi-cal.
- Must meet citizenship or immigration requirements.
- Mothers who are enrolled in other social programs
- Low income.

Check out the website for more vital information below: If not from California check out your local state rules and regulations.

http://www.healthy-families.us/DoIQualify.aspx

The best way to find out what service is best for your child is to contact Medi-cal.

Children's Health Insurance Program (CHIP)

- On Feb. 4, 2009, President Barack Obama signed into law the (**CHIP**) Bill. This bill adds an estimated 4 million eligible low-income children to the existing government sponsored Health Insurance Program, coverage.

- The bill adds nearly $33 billion dollars of enhanced Matching Federal Funds to the State Bill, (**CHIP**). This program will insure 11 million more children in the lower-income family group. They will be covered in the categories of medical, dental, and mental.

- Today there are more than 45 million people without medical insurance. This is a crisis that has exploded in our faces. There isn't an easy fix for this very complex problem.

- The signing of this Children's Bill is the first step in changing the medical insurance system for the needy.

County Medical Service Program (CMPS) or (CMS)

Requirements:

- Age - 21 through 64.

- Reside - in a participating county.

- Low Incomes.

- Not eligible for Medi-Cal.
- Must be a United States Citizen Or have legal immigration status.
- Low-income changes that may affect your eligibility must be reported to your caseworker.
- **Medical Providers do not like to take on (CMS) patients for several reasons:**
    1. Low reimbursement.
    2. The tremendous amount of paperwork involved by their billing staff to get paid for services rendered.

Pharmacy Benefits

- Refer back to the beginning of this chapter under Medi-cal adults.
- (**CMS**) runs under the same guidelines as Medi-cal.
- Sometimes some medication is covered by Medi-cal and will not be covered by (**CMS**).
- When a drug is not covered by (**CMS**) the Pharmacist can send a Pre- Authorization Request to (**CMS)** for approval.
- Your drug may or not be approved at this time.

- **Suggestion:** You always have the option of asking your doctor for free samples.

When you are inquiring into the Medi-Cal and (CMS) system, they are very specific on the documentation they want you to bring with you on your appointment date.

Documents Required:

- A copy of all the receipts of your income for the past three months.
- A copy of all your bank statements.
- A copy of all your rent receipts.
- Driver's License
- Social Security Card.
- Call first they may ask for other documentation.
- Never try and hide your assets. They are in control of software systems that will uncover any income you have hidden.
- Never throw away your old (**CMS**) card or your plastic Medi-Cal card. Your cards are your monthly proof of eligibility.

Chapter 4

Medicare and Tricare

Medicare:

Part A - Inpatient Hospital

- This is for inpatient hospital care. This means the patient has been admitted to the hospital for more than a 24-hour period.
- It also covers medical equipment.
- There is no monthly premium for those who have accumulated at least 40 quarters or ten years of Medicare-covered employment.

Part B – Outpatient

- This accounts for all outpatient activity including doctor's visits, laboratory, x-ray, ambulance transport, etc.
- If you choose to enroll in Part B, the payment will be taken out of your social security check each month or can be deducted from your checking account.

- You need to make a decision on which kind of Medicare meets your specific needs.

Part C or Advantage Plan:

- This plan used to be called Medicare + Choice or Medicare Part C.

- It combines Part A and Part B and may include Part D. (Pharmacy) this will be addressed under Medicare Part D.

- There are many Advantage plans to choose from which varies from state to state.

- The Advantage Plans covers the same services the original Medicare covers.

- Some may include drugs, vision, and dental.

- There will probably be extra charges for these extra services. The plan works like a (**HMO**) or a (**PPO**) which are described in detail in (Chapter 4).

- In addition to your Part B premium which is paid to Medicare, there may or may not be an additional monthly premium payable to the Advantage Plan itself.

- This is usually the cheapest way to go. You pay a small co-pay for visits and medicines (higher for brand name drugs), but with your prescription drugs generally included in this plan, it is a great help.

As with all insurance coverage, some medications are not covered on this plan. You must be aware of this, if you are to apply for one of these plans.

Medicare and Medi-cal Crossover

- When you have Medicare and Medi-cal Insurance you do not have to pay out of pocket expenses in most cases.
- Medicare is billed first since this is your primary insurance. Either by paper claim form or electronically.
- Then Medi-cal is billed either electronically or by paper claim form.
- Part D Pharmacy when you have Medicare and Medi-cal, you may or may not have to pay for part of your prescription.

Part D - Prescription Drug Plans

- The Medicare Part D program was created in 2003 under the Medicare Prescription **Drug, Improvement and Modernization Act of 2003.** It was implemented in January 2006.

- The Part D Coverage is purchased separately under several different plans offered by private companies.

- The enrollment runs from November 15 – December 31 of each year. At this time you are free to change your plan.

- Part D coverage is on a four-tier program.

- There are several ways to purchase your drug plan. The whole idea for you to purchase Part D is to save money when purchasing a prescription drug.

- The specific amount of money you need to spend to reach the gap or donut hole varies from plan to plan. When you reach approximately $2,510 you have reached the donut hole.

- It is a hole you literally have to crawl out of financially. You will now have to start paying 100% of the total cost of your prescription drugs.

- While you are in the donut hole you must still pay your monthly drug premium, which differs, depending upon which company you contract with.

- When your drug costs reach approximately $4,050.00 the insurance will again pay a part of the prescription depending on the drug company you sign up with.

- Your cost for a generic drug is much less than a preferred drug or brand name. Some drugs are not on the plan as described earlier. Be sure to check this out.

- The charge can be much higher depending on the price of the drug. Each year your account starts fresh.

- To help with the Medigap or donut hole problem, which is enormous, many drug stores have started discount cards, Pharmaceutical Company Programs, and State Programs to provide much needed assistance.

Part A & B - Straight Medicare with a Secondary Insurance

- Medicare has many plans. There is still straight Medicare which entitles you to go to any Medical Provider without a referral.

- After an annual deductible, Medicare will pay 80% of the approved rate, but other Medicare rules also apply.

- When you have straight Medicare, you usually want to have a Medigap Policy or a secondary insurance to pick up the 20% that is the patient's responsibility.

- One of the most popular is a program offered through **AARP**.

- On the **AARP** website are many articles about Medicare. This is a good website to browse at your leisure. **http://www.aarp.org**

- In addition, the Medicare website **http://www.medicare.gov** has numerous appeals forms. (Enter "appeals forms" in the search box after you get to the site.) **Check It Out.**

- When you involve (the Social Security Administration), (**SSA**) there is additional stress. However, the staff generally tries to be helpful, especially if you call during less busy times.

- Medicare as we know it may change. I hope it does not become any more complicated to understand than it is right now.

To follow: Professional Example # 2

Appealing Medicare Claims

I was working in a multi doctor's office, doing follow-up on Medicare claims which had been denied. I am telling this story for several reasons. For one thing, Medicare is government insurance. The rules and regulations attached to this insurance is endless.

This Medicare story is about straight Medicare, not an (**HMO)** or (**PPO)**.

When Medicare denies certain (**CPT**) codes, an Appeal Letter needed to be written and mailed to Medicare. All appeals are taken directly from the Medicare Explanation of Benefits (**EOB**).

When Medicare received the appeal letters all the doctor's claims were then paid. In the meantime, the patient always received a copy of the Medicare (**EOB**) and called the office to complain about why only a portion of their bill got paid and not the whole thing. They were reading from the (**EOB**). The (**CPT**) code was paid on a line to line basis.

They had never received a bill from the doctor's office because it was not the patient's responsibility for the balance due on the bill.

If the Medical Provider's office does its job properly, the claim can be appealed properly, and the less time and money you, the patient, will have to spend.

Tricare Insurance

Requirements:

- This military government insurance is mainly for the dependents of the Army, Navy, Marines, Air force, Coast Guard, Public Health Service, and the National Oceanic and Atmospheric Administration.

- It is run by the computer named **DEERS**.

- When you become Medicare eligible, it becomes Tricare for Life.

- There are three popular plans. Tricare Prime, Tricare Extra, Tricare Standard. Tricare used to be called Champus over 10 years ago.

www.military.com/benefits/tricare/tricare-eligibility. It gives all the information you need to know about Tricare and their different plans.

To follow: Personal Example # 3

My Surgery Billing Catastrophe

I was a Navy dependent (spouse) for 30 years. During this time I learned tricks in using Tricare insurance for myself and for my children. I used Tricare at a large Military Hospital and I also used it as Tricare Prime which is an **(HMO)** for private Medical Providers.

When I used the hospital, there was rarely ever any cost to me for any medical care or prescription drugs.

But when I used Tricare Prime as an (**HMO**), I was charged a co-pay for Medical Providers and prescription drugs.

This is one of the horror stories I had to deal with in order to get a surgery paid correctly.

This was back when Tricare was called Champus. I underwent a particular surgery during the same month my husband changed his military status from, "**Active** to **Retired**", to take effect at the end of the month. At that time, all his personal information was changed in the computer system.

Now you may be asking why and how this could affect my surgery getting paid correctly.

When my medical bills were submitted for payment to Champus, there were many hospital charges, assistant surgeon, anesthesiologists, and others.

As a spouse of an, "**Active**" military person, my bills were to be paid at 80% of the contracted rate. They were to be paid out at this rate, since my husband was still active until the end of the month. However, because he changed his status to "**Retired**" in this month, the computer did not work in my favor. Champus called it "a computer glitch."

They paid all of my Medical Providers but not at 80%. The bills were all paid at 75%, the rate for retired personnel.

Needless to say, this small percentage difference made a huge difference in the amount of money I was to pay my Medical Providers from my own pocket.

I immediately called Champus. They explained I needed to write an overwrite letter for each of the individual Medical Providers, explaining the problem, and asking for the payment to be re-adjusted with the proper payment and mailed to them.

This might sound easy but it became the biggest nightmare. I wrote all the letters three times. The insurance company said it never received the first two sets of letters.

Then the third set of letters had to go through all kinds of internal people in different departments. I made many phone calls! After a few months and a lot of stress, the payments were adjusted and the Medical Providers were finally paid correctly, **Hurrah!**

To follow: Personal Example # 4

Surgery, Hospital Screwed Up Bill

I had surgery in a hospital surgical center. To cover this, I had Tricare insurance and never received a bill from this facility. I thought everything was fine and didn't give it another thought until four years later, when I received a bill from the hospital surgical center for $5,000.

How could this be? I was outraged at what was going on. I'd had insurance then, had I not? I even worked in medical insurance billing.

After a phone call to Tricare, I found out what happened. For some reason, my bill had gotten caught on a computer "glitch". Tricare being government insurance, every few years it changes the insurance company which funds their money. It is more complicated than that, but I do not want to get too technical.

My bill got caught on an insurance company change. It was in a different computer system. The check was hanging out in the system, but they could not print it. They also informed me that they could not write a check either.

This error was discovered when an employee was auditing the outstanding open balances in the outpatient surgery center four years later.

I called the supervisor of the billing department. I explained my dilemma, stating that my surgery **was authorized ahead of time.** I would never have been able to walk through their doors without the authorization. This was their screw-up and I wanted this $5,000 charge adjusted off. End of story.

My story was taken before a board that met monthly. It seems I was not the only dissatisfied patient and it was written off. Miracles do happen and I did not even have to write a letter.

To follow: Professional example # 5

Working on Doctor's Billing

I was working for a single Medical Provider, auditing his accounts. In simple words, I was going over each account and trying to find out why an individual account still had an open balance and had never been paid by the patient's medical insurance, or if it had been paid correctly.

I was working on a particular account, where the story was so extraordinary that I still remember it to this day.

A woman was the spouse of an active navy military man. She ended up in the hospital. The doctor I was working for became her Primary Care Provider (**PCP**) and saw her in the hospital many times.

During her stay it became apparent she had a problem that only could be addressed at a certain hospital with that particular specialty. She was transferred there for specialized care.

As a billing person, it was my job to do several things. I needed the medical records of her hospital stay in the hospital where she was under my doctor's care and the identification number (**ID#**) of her spouse (the guarantor). This is the number the spouse uses, when she is issued her military identification card (usually her husband's social security number). This now becomes her Tricare billing identification number.

I had requested her medical records and (**ID#**) from the hospital where she was an inpatient while the doctor I was working for was on her case. That was not a problem, since he was her (**PCP**).

But it became complicated when Tricare had a computer glitch regarding her being in two different hospitals.

Tricare demanded medical records from both hospitals before they would pay anything on this woman's bill.

It was when I called the other hospital to retrieve her medical records that another problem arose. The problem was **Patient Confidentiality.** Even though she had been a former patient, she now no longer was. The doctor had never seen her at the new medical facility.

I could not reach this lady by phone I needed her to sign a Medical Release Form. But it had been at least six months since she was in the hospital and she seemed to have vanished off the face of the earth. The only way I had to clear her account was to turn her over to a Collection Agency. I did not want to do this, yet.

I called the first hospital where she had been a patient when my doctor had been treating her. I asked the billing office if they had ever been paid.

They had billed Tricare and received their Explanation Of Benefits denial. They never tried to appeal for payment. The situation was too complicated. They just turned her over to a collection agency within 90 days from her date of service (**DOS**).

I did not want to turn her over to a collection agency for several reasons: The doctor I work for hired me to bring in the money. I knew he deserved to be paid for services rendered, but because of the medical records, it might not happen.

I called the second hospital back, and spoke to the billing lady. I explained the dilemma I was in, that all I wanted was the patient's hospital medical records for billing purposes only.

The billing lady extended me a professional courtesy, supplying me with her medical records, and Tricare paid us. Wow! What an ordeal.

I'm sure you see the difference in large Medical Providers and small office providers. The small office will go the extra mile. The doctor wants to get paid.

Chapter 5

Medical Computer

Generated Information

Computer Data Step by Step

- You have concluded your medical examination. You are now in your provider's computer system.
- The data will include your personal information.
- Medical insurance information.
- Your charges are compiled and keyed into the computer.
- The next step is to generate from the computer an insurance claim form.
- This form has all the pertinent information that is requested by your insurance company to pay your claim.
- This Claim Form can be a paper claim or can be transmitted electronically.

Filling Out the Claim Form:

- The patient's name.
- The patient's Date Of Birth. (**DOB**)
- Date of Service (**DOS**), meaning the day you were seen.
- The patient's identification number (**ID#**). This is the number printed on your medical insurance card.
- The name of the Guarantor (name of person insured)
- Each individual doctor also has a computer identification number. National Provider Identification Number (**NPI**)
- Each individual facility has a computer identification number. E**xample**: Hospital, doctor's office.
- The (**CPT)** Code. **Example**: Surgery which will have a dollar amount.
- Your diagnosis is assigned a different code of procedure known as (**ICD**) code. If you have three different problems, each will be assigned a separate (**ICD**) code number.

- Place of Service (**POS**). This is where you were seen. **Example**: A doctor's office, hospital, or laboratory.

- The referral number is assigned to you for your medical visit to your Medical Provider by your insurance company or Primary Care Provider (**PCP**).

- The authorization number is assigned to you from your medical insurance company or doctor's office in order to receive treatment. **Example**: An x-ray.

- Your medical insurance company's name and billing address will also be included on the form.

The information on this Claim Form is either mailed to your insurance company or transmitted electronically. It is only good if the person keying in the information, into the computer, is accurate or, the information the patient gives is also accurate.

See sample claim form below:

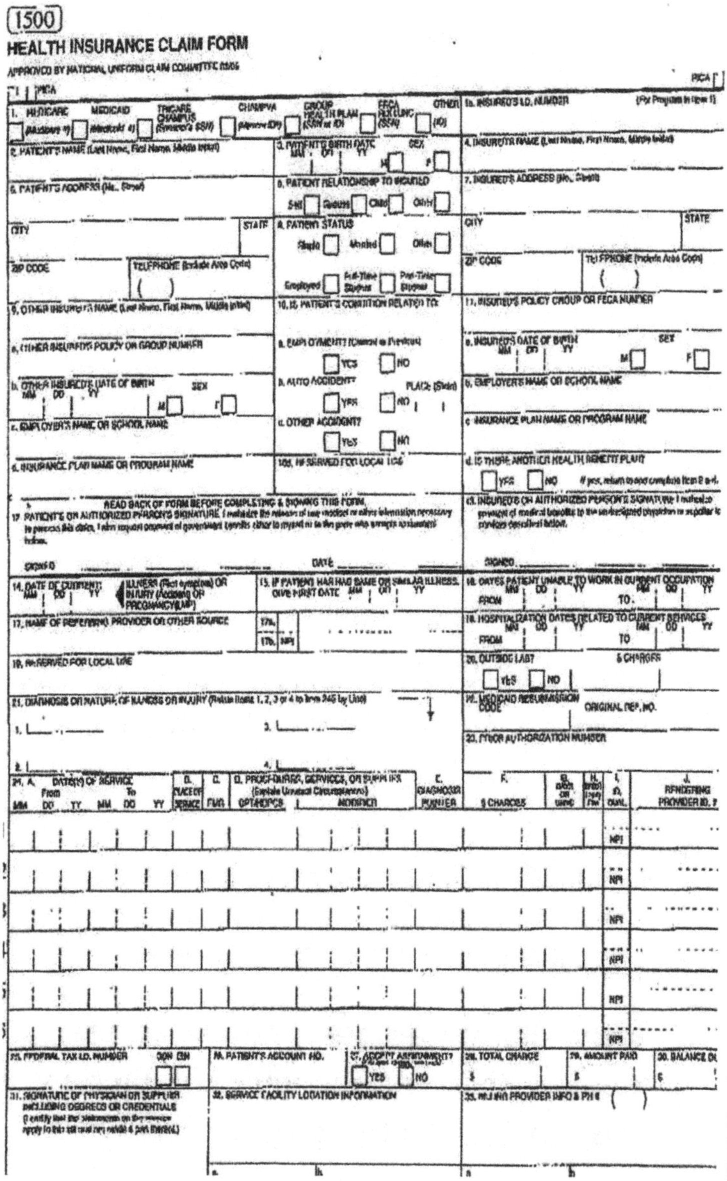

1500

HEALTH INSURANCE CLAIM FORM

APPROVED BY NATIONAL UNIFORM CLAIM COMMITTEE 08/05

PICA

1. MEDICARE MEDICAID TRICARE CHAMPUS CHAMPVA GROUP HEALTH PLAN FECA BLK LUNG OTHER

1a. INSURED'S I.D. NUMBER (For Program in Item 1)

2. PATIENT'S NAME (Last Name, First Name, Middle Initial)

3. PATIENT'S BIRTH DATE MM DD YY SEX M F

4. INSURED'S NAME (Last Name, First Name, Middle Initial)

5. PATIENT'S ADDRESS (No., Street)

6. PATIENT RELATIONSHIP TO INSURED Self Spouse Child Other

7. INSURED'S ADDRESS (No., Street)

CITY STATE

8. PATIENT STATUS Single Married Other

CITY STATE

ZIP CODE TELEPHONE (Include Area Code) ( )

Employed Full-Time Student Part-Time Student

ZIP CODE TELEPHONE (Include Area Code) ( )

9. OTHER INSURED'S NAME (Last Name, First Name, Middle Initial)

10. IS PATIENT'S CONDITION RELATED TO:

11. INSURED'S POLICY GROUP OR FECA NUMBER

a. OTHER INSURED'S POLICY OR GROUP NUMBER

a. EMPLOYMENT? (Current or Previous) YES NO

a. INSURED'S DATE OF BIRTH MM DD YY SEX M F

b. OTHER INSURED'S DATE OF BIRTH MM DD YY SEX M F

b. AUTO ACCIDENT? YES NO PLACE (State)

b. EMPLOYER'S NAME OR SCHOOL NAME

c. EMPLOYER'S NAME OR SCHOOL NAME

c. OTHER ACCIDENT? YES NO

c. INSURANCE PLAN NAME OR PROGRAM NAME

d. INSURANCE PLAN NAME OR PROGRAM NAME

10d. RESERVED FOR LOCAL USE

d. IS THERE ANOTHER HEALTH BENEFIT PLAN? YES NO If yes, return to and complete item 9 a-d.

READ BACK OF FORM BEFORE COMPLETING & SIGNING THIS FORM.

12. PATIENT'S OR AUTHORIZED PERSON'S SIGNATURE

SIGNED DATE

13. INSURED'S OR AUTHORIZED PERSON'S SIGNATURE

SIGNED

14. DATE OF CURRENT: ILLNESS (First symptom) OR INJURY (Accident) OR PREGNANCY(LMP)

15. IF PATIENT HAS HAD SAME OR SIMILAR ILLNESS. GIVE FIRST DATE MM DD YY

16. DATES PATIENT UNABLE TO WORK IN CURRENT OCCUPATION FROM TO

17. NAME OF REFERRING PROVIDER OR OTHER SOURCE 17a. 17b. NPI

18. HOSPITALIZATION DATES RELATED TO CURRENT SERVICES FROM TO

19. RESERVED FOR LOCAL USE

20. OUTSIDE LAB? YES NO $ CHARGES

21. DIAGNOSIS OR NATURE OF ILLNESS OR INJURY (Relate Items 1, 2, 3 or 4 to Item 24E by Line)

1. 2. 3. 4.

22. MEDICAID RESUBMISSION CODE ORIGINAL REF. NO.

23. PRIOR AUTHORIZATION NUMBER

24. A. DATE(S) OF SERVICE From To MM DD YY MM DD YY | B. PLACE OF SERVICE | C. EMG | D. PROCEDURES, SERVICES, OR SUPPLIES (Explain Unusual Circumstances) CPT/HCPCS MODIFIER | E. DIAGNOSIS POINTER | F. $ CHARGES | G. DAYS OR UNITS | H. EPSDT Family Plan | I. ID. QUAL. | J. RENDERING PROVIDER ID. #

NPI
NPI
NPI
NPI
NPI
NPI

25. FEDERAL TAX I.D. NUMBER SSN EIN

26. PATIENT'S ACCOUNT NO.

27. ACCEPT ASSIGNMENT? YES NO

28. TOTAL CHARGE $

29. AMOUNT PAID $

30. BALANCE DUE $

31. SIGNATURE OF PHYSICIAN OR SUPPLIER INCLUDING DEGREES OR CREDENTIALS

32. SERVICE FACILITY LOCATION INFORMATION

a. b.

33. BILLING PROVIDER INFO & PH # ( )

a. b.

Chapter 6

Important Phone Calls

When you receive a bill from your Medical Provider now is the time for you to call your Medical Provider's office and ask them the following questions: (See Chapter 1 Audit).

- Was my account audited?
- Has it been billed correctly?
- Has it been paid correctly?
- Has the secondary insurance been billed? (see Chapter 1, under Secondary Insurance)
- Has the secondary insurance paid?
- Has the adjustment been made correctly?
- Does this claim need to be appealed?
- **If the claim has been appealed and denied, the balance will usually be moved over to the patient's responsibility.**

What do you do when you receive your Explanation of Benefits (EOB) from your Medical Insurance Company denying payment?

- There are many reasons for the denial of your medical claims. First of all, as you open your Explanation Of Benefits (**EOB**) from your insurance company you will find out if it was paid or not.

- The (**EOB**) you just received in the mail contains:

  1. The patients name.
  2. A detailed report as to the Date of Service (**DOS**).
  3. The address where you were seen. Place of Service (**POS**).
  4. What Medical Provider you saw.
  5. Total amount of the bill.
  6. Your Diagnosis (**ICD**) code.
  7. It will also state what was not paid and why.
  8. This is called the **(CPT)** code. The reason for the visit and a dollar amount. The (**CPT**) code is paid line by line.

9. **Example:** You had surgery. During that surgery there were several procedures performed called (**CPT**) codes. This is why if you ever received an itemized hospital bill it can be pages long.

10. The insurance company may not have paid on any of the (**CPT**) code lines or it may have paid some and not paid others. This is why you have to read the (**EOB**) very carefully to find out what they did or did not pay.

- Chances are you still will not understand the reasons for the denial. In the following are some suggestions on how to proceed.

- Appeal information will be on the Explanation of Benefits.

Read Your Contract

- You must understand your insurance contract.

- **Read it**. Find out what is and what is not covered.

- **Call Your Insurance Company** and ask them to explain anything you do not understand in the language you do understand.

Your Direct Responsibility:

- Co-pays
- Non-covered services (Sometimes this can be questioned.)
- Deductibles
- Your policy's percentage of the allowable amount. This corresponds with the contracted rate between your Medical Provider and your medical insurance.
- All these items are listed on your (**EOB**).
- This is the way your insurance company pays your claim without any money changing hands. **Meaning**, the money will be applied to your deductible.
- The Medical Provider will not receive any payment until you have met your deductible requirements first.

Information Insurance Company Needs:

- Copy of your insurance card.
- Copy of your Explanation of Benefits (**EOB**)
- Your name and the patient's name (may not be the same).

- Your Identification Number (**ID#**) - the number on your insurance card.

- The date of service (**DOS**).

- The name of your Medical Provider.

- Place of Service.

- When you receive the information from your insurance company about this particular bill, you will now know what your options are.

Call Your Medical Provider's Office

- **Calm down** if you are upset. Explain to the billing person about your telephone call to your insurance company and what they have said. Don't forget to keep a phone log of the conversation.

- The billing person will look up your bill in their computer system.

- It should have the reason for the denial listed, or they can find a copy of your (**EOB**) and see for themselves.

- You and your provider must decide the next step. After all, your provider's office wants to receive payment for services rendered.

- Record your phone call.

- If possible, tell them you are recording them.

The provider may say this claim was billed correctly. Therefore, you are responsible for the balance of your bill.

Chapter 7

10+ Reasons for Denial

Insurance Forms

- Not filling out forms which were sent by your insurance company completely or at all for that matter.
- Not returning the forms to your insurance company.
- Without the forms your insurance will not pay your bill.
- Your insurance only wants to know if there is any other insurance to bill. **Example**: Car Insurance

Timely Filing

- Meaning the claim form needs to be submitted to your insurance company prior to time limit.
- Each insurance company has different time limits.

Wrong Address - Insurance Company Billed

- When the wrong Medical Insurance Company was billed.

- Mailed to wrong address of the same insurance company.

Medical Necessity

- This is one of the most common reasons for a medical bill to be denied.

- The insurance companies are becoming very choosy on what they consider medically necessary.

- This type of denial will need to be addressed by the doctor's billing staff.

- If the appeal was denied, it could end up needing to be taken a step further, by appealing it yourself. (See sample letters in chapter 9)

Human Error

- Even though I have mentioned many reasons for medical bills to be denied, I think human error is a very large part of the problem. When information is keyed into the computer, an error may occur.

Eligibility

- Many times the patient changes medical insurance.
- This can be within the same insurance plan.
- It could change from an (**HMO**) to a (**PPO**) and you are not aware of it.
- **Be Aware, read and know your plan.**
- If you had Blue Cross and change to Aetna, for example, this is a huge change.
- Maybe you did inform your Medical Provider.
- The information was never changed in their computer system.
- Your medical insurance claim will be mailed or electronically transmitted to your old insurance carrier and be denied: "Not eligible."
- This can usually be handled by a phone call to your Medical Provider's billing office.
- Make sure, while you have a human person on the line, that the change is made.
- Write on your phone log the name of the person who you have been talking to and any other notes for reference purposes.

- Once they have changed the information, ask them to please re-bill your insurance company.

- Eligibility may again be denied because your new insurance company has not updated their computer system.

- In all walks of life, the computer generates and controls all areas of the business world.

A Live Human Being sits at their computer and keys in your personal information. Until this has been done correctly, you will not be eligible. Computers don't make mistakes, humans do.

Misplaced Paperwork

- Medical Providers are notorious for misplacing a copy of your medical insurance card.

- The reason for this is simple. If your medical chart is not available to a specific person (a medical insurance biller or bookkeeper) at the time your card is being copied, it will get placed in a pile of filing for "**Whenever**." Meanwhile, your insurance needs to be billed and the computer was not updated.

- This can cause problems such as the wrong insurance being billed, especially if your medical insurance has been changed in any manner. **Example**: Married, or remarried, new medical insurance, new employer, etc. The patient's must have the medical provider's office update the computer.

Lost Payment

- Try to avoid paying by cash. Receipts get lost.
- When you, the patient, or your insurance company makes a payment to your Medical Provider, in some cases it never gets properly entered into the computer system under your account number.
- The money could have been applied to another patient's account.
- This happens frequently.
- If there isn't any documentation of a payment for a specific Date of Service (**DOS**), you will have to show a copy of the front and back of the check, or the receipt which was given at the time a payment was made.

To follow: Personal Example # 6

Lost Co-pay

I recently received a bill from a Medical Specialist for a charge of $5.00. The letter also said that I could now consider myself in pre-collection status. I had been to see this specialist two times. Both times I paid my co-pay. My co-pay was $5.00. I always pay my co-pays for the specific reason I will explain to you now.

I called the specialist's office and asked to speak to the person handling the medical insurance. I explained to the woman that I paid my co-pay on the date of my visit and received a receipt. I asked her to look in her receipt book under the date of service (**DOS**) in question. I could hear in her voice that she was very, very put out, but she said she would do it, although it would take a few days.

I received a call back within the hour. She was very nice and said she found the receipt for $5.00 and the money was not put into my account, but went into somebody else's.

I was happy to resolve this ridiculous mistake, but at the same time, when I received the letter I was furious. All of this stress, including a threat of being put into a collection agency, for a $5.00 co-pay charge.

Reasons for Denials Continued:

Therapy Visits

- Insurance companies may limit the number of therapy visits you are allowed.

- In many cases, getting the authorization extended to allow more visits was allowed to slip through the cracks.

- Maybe you were seen for more visits than were authorized within a specific time frame.

- You, the patient, must be aware of how many visits were authorized and how many were used.

- When it is time to extend the visits, make sure they were extended by the therapist.

- Oral Authorization is another way your insurance will not pay for your therapy. This is when the therapist called and received an oral authorization (over the phone).

- There wasn't any written document follow-up, or no oral confirmation numbers generated for this specific authorization.

- Your insurance company can later turn around and say they never authorized this treatment. They didn't have a record.

- The therapist needs to ask your insurance to fax a confirmation in a very short 1 - or 2 - sentence authorization, either before or after it has been confirmed orally over the phone. In this way, your physical therapist will have the authorization on hand.

Surgery Insurance Horrors

Scheduled Surgery

- The patient usually does not need to get involved with the scheduling of his or her own surgery.

- However, there are some facts that are not revealed until after the Explanation Of Benefits (**EOBs**) from your insurance company start pouring in.

- When you have surgery, you go to a hospital, or surgery center.

- In addition to the surgeon, there is an assistant surgeon (required by state law), anesthesiologists, probable laboratory samples, and x-rays. There may be more charges but these are the most usual.

- What you, the patient, need to understand is this: Your surgery and facility (hospital or surgery center) will have been approved by your medical insurance.

- The rest of the Medical Providers' insurance are not pre-approved.

- The assistant surgeon's service **should be** approved in advance.

- You will be able to find out if this was approved by calling your Surgeon's office or your Medical Insurance.
- The rest of the Medical Providers listed may be out-of-network.
- This means you will be paying much more for your surgery than you would if all of your Medical Providers were on your insurance plan.
- This situation happens over and over again. The patient is the last to find out until the bills start pouring in.

Emergency Surgery

- When you have an Emergency Surgery your medical insurance is really in jeopardy.
- The Hospital where you were taken by ambulance may be out-of-network.
- The surgeon may be out-of-network.
- The assisted surgeon and all the other specialists' may be out-of-network.

  The only thing you have going for you is this was an emergency. This may need to be appealed by your medical providers and then you may have to appeal. (See Appeal Letters in Chapter 9)

- When you appeal, you can use your contract for reference in your letter. When you read this book in its entirety, you should be able to understand your contract better. When the insurance companies respond in writing to you, in most cases they are quoting your contract to you, on a line-by-line basis.

To follow: Professional Example # 7

Eligibility Mix Ups

I woman I know received a denied **(EOB)** from her Medical Insurance Company for a doctor's visit.

As she read the (**EOB**) over, she realized her ex-husband's name and identification number were not on the paper. She immediately realized what had happened.

When she checked into her new doctor's office, and her personal information was added, the part of the Insurance Guarantor (the person who is actually insured), her name was added, not her ex-husband's. This happened, even though she had told them her ex-husband was the Insurance Guarantor.

This was a simple mistake to fix. The Medical Provider had to update the billing information in their computer system and re-bill her insurance company. End of problem.

Another aspect of this is when the woman checked in with the receptionist, a copy of her insurance card was made that day. It was never placed in the chart.

On further investigation, it was discovered that the copy of the insurance card had been placed in a stack of filing to be done in the future. This immediately set bells ringing in her head. This is not a very organized medical office.

Reasons For Denials Continued:

Unidentified Money

- All Medical Providers receive in their offices checks in which they can't identify the patient.
- The checks can come directly from the patient's insurance company or from the patient.
- Necessary information is not printed on the check to identify the patient.
- The Explanation Of Benefits (**EOB**) becomes disconnected from the check.
- The person that enters this information into the computer will not know who the check belongs to.
- The billing person will now place the check into an unidentified money account.

- You, the patient, will still keep receiving bills from this Medical Provider since the check was not placed into your account.
- When you are trying to track down a payment which you know was made to your Medical Provider, always ask them to check the unidentified money account.
- The Medical Provider's office is always happy to identify money and place it into the correct patients account.

When Medical Providers Appeal First:

Retro Authorization For Surgery Performed

- A patient received an (**EOB**) denial from their insurance company. They were only going to pay for part of a surgery the patient had received. The surgery had become more complicated than anticipated. A second procedure needed to be performed at that time, which was not authorized.
- **Note:** In this particular case, I would now contact the surgeon's office. Speak to the billing person and ask them to ask the insurance company for a retro authorization. (see chapter 1)

- The surgeon's office will have to do their own appeal letter, plus send along all the medical records pertaining to the surgery.

- The outcome of this problem is the patient might have to do their own medical appeal.

Diagnosis Problem

- You may receive an Explanation of Benefits (**EOB)** denial from your medical insurance company, stating:

- Your **(CPT)** code (reason for your visit with a dollar amount) and your (**ICD)** (diagnosis) do not match.

- Payment is denied on your medical bill for this (**DOS**) and this Medical Provider."

- **Example:** A man goes to his Primary Care Physician. This would be for a doctor's visit (**CPT**) code (the reason for the visit plus a dollar value).

- His diagnosis (**ICD**) code was a sore throat.

- The problem occurs when the charges are entered into the computer.

- A diagnose (**ICD**) code for a PAP Smear was entered in error.

- The medical office definitely needs to appeal this bill.

Information In Wrong Account

- When Information entered into the computer is placed into the wrong patient's account.

- This situation can only be handled by the Medical Provider's office. This is why you really need to read your Explanation of Benefits (**EOB**) by the date of service (**DOS**) (this is the date you were seen) and where you were seen. Place of Service (**POS**).

- Once again when information is entered into the computer incorrectly, obvious problems will result.

These are some of the most common reasons the medical insurance companies deny payment. There are many, many more.

Chapter 8

Appealing Your Medical Bills

Never be afraid to appeal your medical insurance. What is the worst thing that can happen? They can deny it again or they can pay it correctly. Go for it!!!

- **Always keep a copy of all documentation you submit to your insurance company for your own records**.

Medical Records

- When you are appealing your claim it is best, in most circumstances, to provide all your medical records pertaining to the specific date of service and the Medical Provider.
- You can receive your medical records by contacting your Medical Provider's office and signing a, Medical Records Release Form.
- Medical insurance companies need your Date Of Service (**DOS**) and Place Of Service (**POS**).

This is how they track all your medical care by each individual provider.

- **Example:** You were seen by your **doctor** that morning in her office. That afternoon you were admitted to the **hospital**. Now you have two different providers on the same day.

- Try to make your appeal letter as professional and personal as possible.

- The person that will be reviewing all your information will expect to see your entire case presentation in one sitting.

- If the Appeal Board needs more information, they will send you a letter, email, or phone you.

- When appealing your claim, pour your emotions and passions out in your letter to the Appeal Board.

- If you do not have a computer to type your letter, handwrite it. Just make sure your writing is easy to read. Sometimes a handwritten letter is even more effective than one that has been created on the computer.

Filing a State Complaint

- Your first appeal was filed and denied, with your insurance company.

- Next, call to speak to the manager within the insurance company. If no positive results and you still feel this an error then:

- It is now time to file a **State Complaint.**

- Contact your State Insurance Department by searching the Internet. **This is not simple as it sounds.**

- Each state has different requirements. I was searching for more specific information, but I found that there are electronic forms set up for different states.

- A website for California is http://ag.ca.gov/consumers/general.php

- There may be forms also which you can print from the website. This will take a little bit of your time. Some states websites maybe harder to find than others. **Hang in there!**

The following information needed:

- The forms are generally self explanatory but be prepared to give the following information:

- The reason you feel this claim should be paid and why it was denied (that is, give the reason for denial that the insurance company provided directly from the Explanation Of Benefits (**EOB**).

- Send a copy of your insurance card or its identification number (**ID#**) if requested.

- Send all your documentation from your original appeal, including the phone log you should be keeping.

- Keep a copy of all documentation.

- If the amount of the claim you are disputing is high, and you cannot come to a satisfactory resolution with your medical insurance company, you may need legal representation.

Insurance Companies also monitor the websites. They keep in touch with consumer complaints.

Consumer Websites

- There are many consumer websites popping up all over the Internet where you can post your medical insurance horror stories. http://www.dca.ca.gov/consumer/complaints.shtml

- These cannot usually solve the problems, but they might add some pressure to the insurance industry, as well as help another person.

Better Business Bureau (BBB)

- Businesses accredited in the United States and Canada.
- This is another place to make a consumer complaint.
- They try to resolve the conflict.
- Business do not have to be accredited by the (**BBB**)

When Payment Issued By Insurance:

- The money is applied to your bill by your date of service.
- It is then adjusted, if an adjustment is necessary.
- The balance remaining is immediately applied to you, the patient.
- You will then receive a bill that states you are now responsible for the balance of the bill.
- Sometimes small balances will be written off.
- If yours wasn't call and ask the providers office to write off the small balance.
- It never hurts to ask.
- Insurance companies have been known to pay part of a (**CPT)** code (is the reason for the visit

with the dollar amount) or not pay one code at all.

- The Explanation of Benefits **(EOB)** has to be read line by line.
- It will say if it was paid, adjusted, or a partial payment made.

If you are confused, call your insurance company. They will explain to you the activity of each line on your (**EOB**).

Your options are:

- You can pay your bill.
- Write a Letter of Appeal.
- Leave the bill unpaid and your credit rating will be affected.
- You may end up in a Collection Agency.
- The final determination is made on your bill when it goes to a Collection Agency.

Chapter 9

Formatting an Appeal Letter

All letters to insurance companies should be in formal block format, (**BF**). Meaning all parts of the letter should be lined up on the left margin except for the heading which is centered at the top of the letter.

Parts of the Letter

- **Letterhead:**

  Patient's full name, line 1, full address, lines 2 and 3. Phone number w/area code, line 4 and finally your email address if you desire on line 5.

- Then come down 6 lines and type current date

- Then come down 4 lines and type, Name and Address of party sending the appeal, if different than the patient appealing. Then double space.

- To the, **Attention Of:** And then type, the name of whom ever sent the initial letter to you, if one was given. If not given, then type the **Departments** name that sent you the initial letter. There after, double space between all future paragraphs.

- **Greeting or Salutation:** (Dear?, The name given or To **Whom It May Concern:)** if name is not given.

- **Introduction Paragraph:** This addresses why you are writing the letter in the first place. Usually one or two sentences.

- **Body of Letter:** The basic information needed to state your case, position, and for identification purposes. This will incorporate a minimum of the following points:

  1. Date of Service in question.

  2. Identification Number (**ID#**)

  3. Amount of the Bill.

  4. Give the reasons why you feel their decision is wrong and why you feel it needs to be either, paid by you, or adjusted.

- **Closing Paragraph:** Usually starts out Thank you for your time and consideration or in closing…

- **Complimentary Closing:** Respectively Submitted: and return 4 lines then,

- Type your name.

- Your **Signature** goes in the 4 spaces provided for (**Oh!** Remember To Sign Your Letter.)

- Your **Title** (if applicable) goes on the line below your typed name.

- **C C,** Meaning, there are Enclosure(s) or Attachment(s), being sent to other person(s) if applicable. **Example**, Attorney

To follow: Professional Example # 8

In the year 2000, I was working in a large hospital billing office. I found that I was one of the few people who could write a proper appeal letter. I put a series of sample letters onto a CD and let the other staff members use them.

I felt really happy when a co-worker came over to me after she had just spoken to an insurance company. The girl on the phone had said to her, "Write your letters like Linda, and you will get paid."

If you feel you cannot write this type of letter, utilize a family member or friend. This is important and it could make all the difference in your claim being paid or not.

To follow: Personal Example # 9

Name
Address
City, State, Zip Code
Phone Number

Blue Cross
Address
City, State, Zip Code

Today's Date

Attention: Medical Appeal Board

To Whom It May Concern:

DOS:

ID#:

Amount of Bill:

I received an Explanation of Benefits (**EOB**) from your company, dated January 1, 2009. On this **(EOB)** the date of service May 6, 2008 was denied as an unauthorized visit to my Orthopedic Surgeon (name?)

I have a copy of my authorization and I am attaching it to this letter, along with a copy of my (**EOB**).

I would appreciate your attention to this matter as soon as possible and I look forward to your response. If appropriate please correct your records and pay this medical bill.

Respectively Submitted,

Your Name

To Follow: Personal Example # 10

Unauthorized Hospital Admission

I received an Explanation of Benefits (**EOB**) from you, dated May 1, 2008. The Date of Service was denied because I did not go to _______ Hospital which is the hospital on my insurance plan.

When I was taken by ambulance to the hospital, I was not breathing. They took me to the closest hospital. When I finally was seen by an emergency room doctor, I was told I was having a heart attack. I was then admitted to the hospital for three days.

I did not have a choice where the ambulance service took me which happened to be the closest hospital available. I came to find out later this hospital was not on my insurance plan.

I am attaching all my medical records from my hospital stay.

I hope you will please re-consider my appeal and pay this bill. Thank you.

To Follow: Personal Example # 11

Out-Of-Network Emergency

On the **(EOB)** dated June 1, 2008, it stated I was out of network for the hospital I was in. I was out of network, but there were extenuating circumstances.

I was involved in a home fire. I was burnt over most of the lower half of my body. My terrified husband bundled me into his car and drove me to the nearest emergency room. This emergency room was on my insurance plan.

When the emergency room doctor examined me, the doctor immediately called an ambulance and had me taken and admitted to a special hospital for burn victims.

You will see by my attached medical records that this is well documented in the emergency room records. I am sorry that this burn hospital was out-of-network, but in this case, I feel my medical bill should be treated as in network and paid properly. This was clearly a medical emergency and I didn't have a choice.

Thank you for your time and consideration in this very traumatic time in my life.

This is part of a letter I wrote for a friend to appeal her medical insurance denial. All the circumstances were accurate as stated. For patient confidentiality, I could not include the complete letter. The amount of the bill was $26,000.

When I met with my friend, I told her I would need for her to call her insurance company and find out if they needed a special form for me to be able to call and speak on her behalf. I call this an authorization to speak on her behalf.

In fact, they did have a special form she needed to fill out and return to her insurance company. She did this as soon as she received the form. She called me and told me on the day she mailed it to please follow up.

I waited two weeks to make sure that not only was it received, but that the information had been updated in their computer

When I telephoned my friends insurance company, I spoke to a young woman. I explained why I was calling and who I was calling for. She checked her computer and said very nicely, “We never received the form.”

I then said to her to go check in the office in the pile of paperwork waiting to be filed or in a stack which needed to be entered into a computer for update. This sort of form would, of course, not be considered high priority.

Miracle of miracles, she came back to the phone with the form in her hands. She entered the information into the computer right then and there, and I was able to speak to her about my friend's insurance bills. The woman told me if I were sending an appeal for this claim, I would need to have it in by a certain date. I thanked her for the information and said the appeal letter would be in by that specific date.

Linda Meckler wrote an Appeal Letter to my
medical insurance company for me.
The result was $26,000 was written off.
I never had to pay a penny.

Robert and Katherine Foster

To Follow: Personal Example # 12

Medical Necessity

I received an explanation of benefits, dated January 1, 2009, for the date of service November 2, 2008. This bill was denied because of lack of medical necessity. I can assure you there was plenty of medical necessity.

I broke my arm and my mother took me to the nearest hospital emergency room. At that time, I had to have surgery to reset my arm, and my arm was placed in a cast.

I am attaching my medical records I received from my emergency room visit. In these records is an x-ray clearly showing the bones that were broken in my arm. It also has the original emergency room report and my operation report. But most importantly, it was the emergency room doctor who declared this an emergency and surgery needed to be addressed, **immediately**.

Please show me, in my policy, where it states that the injury as declared by the doctor, an emergency, which in this case was broken bones and needed to be addressed immediately was denied.

In closing, I am legally requesting you to pay my bill.

Thank you for your time and consideration.

To Follow: Personal Example # 13

Ambulance Transport

On my Explanation Of Benefits (**EOB**), dated January 2, 2009, for the date of service (**DOS**) December 3, 2008, my bill was denied because you said I did not need an ambulance ride.

I can assure you that I fell in my house and could not get up off the floor. When I arrived at the hospital emergency room, I found out my right hip was broken, causing me extreme pain. There is no way I could have gotten to the hospital without using an ambulance.

I have stapled my medical records to this letter including my ambulance report. Please re-evaluate your position on non-payment of this bill and please pay it.

Thank you for your help in this matter.

To Follow: Personal Example # 14

Release Of Medical Records

Attention: Medical Records:

Please release my medical records to me, Your Name), for the dates of service from ________ to __________ .

Please mail them to the above address, or fax them to me in the privacy of my own home. My fax number is______________ .

If you have any questions, please call me at ____________ .

Thank you for the prompt attention to this matter.

To Follow: Personal Example # 15

Letter of Hardship

I am writing this letter because I am unable to pay this medical bill. I am not working because I have a bad heart and can't walk. I need to use a wheelchair. I do not have any means to support my family or myself. I have five kids; my wife is the care giver of me and my children since they are all small and not of school age.

If you require any documentation from me, please let me know what you need and I will provide it for you.

Thank you for the consideration in this matter.

Sincerely,

?

To Follow: Personal Example Letter # 16

Monthly Contract Agreement

I would like to make small monthly payments of $? a month. I hope you accept this amount to be paid monthly. It is all I can afford right now since I am not working.

Please contact me by my phone number or email listed above. Thank you for your attention to this matter.

To Follow: Personal Example # 17

Balance Write Off Letter

I am asking you to write off the balance on my account for dates of service, ___________ and not send it to a collection agency.

I am not working now because I have a major heart condition.

I do not know when I will be able to return to work if ever. Please help me by writing off this balance and accepting the insurance payment as payment in full.

My insurance paid everything except $100.

Thank you very much for your time. I hope you can help me in this situation. I am waiting to hear from you about this matter.

To Follow: Personal Example # 18

Letter of Reduction and Payoff

I am asking you to reduce my bill by 40% and I will pay that amount in full. I am not working and my charge cards have all been maxed out. I do care about my credit rating. I could pay this bill, if you could reduce it by 40%.

Please call me at your earliest convenience. I will have a check to you immediately.

I hope you will consider my offer to pay off this medical bill at the discounted rate.

Thank you for your help.

To Follow: Personal Example # 19

Cease and Desist Letter

This letter is to inform you to cease and desist the harassing phone calls you have been making to my home the last two months.

I do not appreciate this form of harassment. If I could afford to pay off this bill or make payments I would.

Please also remove the $35.00 a month late fee from my account from the past and for the future.

I have been out of work for a year. Disability only goes so far.

See Chapter 11 for more information.

To Follow: Personal Example Letter: # 20

Authorization To Discuss Medical Records

I, (Person's Name) give permission to (name of Medical Provider, etc) to discuss my medical care and medical bills with (the name of the person or institution.)

(Your signature) ____________________

Some medical insurance companies have their own forms they want you to use. Call and ask them which they prefer, to save time and confusion.

Chapter 10

How to Submit Your Medical Appeals

Each Envelope Should Contain:

- Your signed appeal letter.
- A Copy of all your medical records pertaining to this Medical Provider and Date of Service (**DOS).**
- A copy of your Explanation of Benefits (**EOB).**
- Phone Log.
- A copy of your insurance card.

Mailing Tips:

- Call your insurance company. Tell them you are sending an appeal letter.
- Find out the address because it will be different from the insurance company's regular address in most cases.
- Find out the date the Appeal needs to be in the Appeals Board Hand for timely filing.

- Try to find out a person's name to send it to, if possible.

- Always mail your appeal letters with all documentation in an envelope big enough that the paperwork can stay flat instead of being folded.

- Take the envelope directly to the post office and send it, "**Certified Registered, Return, Receipt.**"

- In this way you have a receipt with the date it was sent, and it will have to be signed for when it gets to the recipient's address.

- With every appeal you send, you should send them each, in separate envelops, along with the appeal letter and medical records for that Date Of Service (**DOS**).

- This is not only for tracking purposes but if you have more than one appeal several different people will be receiving them.

- Get each one, "**Certified Registered Return, Receipt** separately**.**

- Everybody wants to save money, especially in this severe recession time. But saving money on copying, envelopes, and postage is not the place to scrimp, especially if there is a large amount of money to recoup, at stake.

Faxing Tips:

- Fax machines are very common, but if you do not have your own personal fax machine, it's worth asking a friend if you may use theirs. Or go to Kinko's, Staples, etc. for a small fee they can fax your documents for you.

- Always call the medical insurance company first and speak to a claims adjuster.

- Explain you are submitting an appeal letter, with your medical records as documentation.

- Ask if it would be appropriate to fax the documentation instead of using the mail.

- If the answer is "yes," get all the information you need for completing your fax cover sheet.

- Get a specific person's name and department. Get whatever information you need to get the fax to the correct person.

- Do not forget to put all your personal information on the cover sheet.

- By this I mean your name, the patient's name (if different), (**DOS**), how many pages the fax will be, and today's date.

- Pages have a way of becoming disconnected, especially if there are several pages.

- All you will have is the confirmation sheet from the fax machine, stating a fax was sent, where, what day and time.

- Make sure the fax cover letter also States, "**Medical Appeal Letter**."

- Wait about 15 minutes and call the person you faxed it to. In a large office there may only be two fax machines used by several people.

- Unless a certain person is waiting for a specific fax, that person may not receive the fax for days, if ever.

- When you hear from the person you faxed your medical appeal to, "Yes, I received it and there were 20 pages," you can breathe a sigh of relief. It has arrived, and arrived in the correct place.

- You can even ask the person who received your appeal envelope to fax you back a confirmation of their receiving the appeal.

- Make sure to keep a phone log of all your correspondence and conversations with the insurance company and Medical Providers' offices. Add this latest information to your notes, immediately.

- Medical Providers' offices use the fax as often as they can when sending medical appeals. It is faster and they do not have to make a possibly inconvenient, quick trip to the post office to have the envelope mailed "**Certified, Registered Return, Receipt**."

- Never forget about patient confidentiality. Your personal data on a fax will be exposed to more people than when it is received by mail. You have to remember when submitting anything to an insurance company, several people are privy to your information, faxed or mailed.

E-Mail Tips:

- This requires a scanner.
- Call your medical insurance company and get the correct e-mail address plus a name.
- Follow up with a phone call to make sure the person you e-mailed your appeal to has actually received it.
- Have this person send you a confirming e-mail to that effect.
- Which ever way you choose to go, get it there before the Appeal Boards date of review of your case.

The people that review these appeals do not just review yours. They review hundreds a week. Their eyes get tired and they want to read as little as possible. Get to the point! Using larger font may push your letter further up the pile.

In conclusion, having worked in many medical billing offices, I have found that most of the medical office staff, who create the Appeal Letters for their Medical Providers, cannot write a proper Appeal Letter. This is why it is so important to take the time to write your letter correctly.

Chapter 11

The Collection Agency

- If you do not pay your medical bill, in most cases you will be turned over to a collection agency.
- This is where the interest starts adding up on your account.
- Your account will also be reported to all three credit bureaus.

The collection agency will ask you the following questions:

- Can you make large monthly payments?
- Can you refinance your home?
- Can you borrow money from a family member or a friend to pay off your bill?

Asking for a Discount

- Often asking for a discount on your bill works.

- **Remember,** You need the pay off money available to pay off the discount total within a very short period of time.

- When you do not have medical insurance, or when your medical insurance has paid its portion and left you with a large balance you can often proceed to negotiate for a lower balance total and then make payments.

- When Medical Insurance is involved; the provider sometimes will not discount your bill. Always ask. You will never know the answer to this question unless you ask.

Always make sure your insurance was billed and paid properly. Make sure the balance is definitely your responsibility and above all, get a signed receipt on any payments made.

Note: Many times when an account ends up in a collection agency it has never been billed to your medical insurance. This happens most often in large billing offices or in hospitals.

Collection Agency Harassment

- If the collection agency is calling you daily and driving you crazy, you can write a "Certified, Return Receipt" letter. In this letter ask them to,

"Cease and Desist" their phone calls. Contact me by mail only.

- According to the law in California the collection agency is only allowed one phone call to your residence per day and its employees are not allowed to call at unreasonable hours.

- **The rules and laws may vary from state to state, but the nastier "junkyard dog" agencies do not care about federal or state laws. They are sometimes calling from an offshore location, such as Jamaica or Costa Rica.**

- With the, "Cease and Desist" order in place, the collection agency can continue to the next step.

- Also, you can go the next step, seek out legal advice.

Legal Action

Before legal action is taken by your collection agency they need to know the answers to the following questions:

- Do you own your own home?

- Do you own your own business?

- Are you employed?
- By whom are you employed?
- Collection Agencies can take you to court:
- Have a lien placed upon your property.
- Garnish your wages from your employment in certain instances.

You do not have to divulge any information asked by the collection agency. Legal advice may now be necessary. Legal expenses will add heavily to your already interest laden bill.

Bureaus Listed Below:

Experian

P.O. Box 2002, Allen, TX 75013 888-397-3742

Equifax

P.O. Box 740241, Atlanta, GA 30374 800-685-1111

TransUnion

P.O. Box 1000, Chester, PA 19022 800-888-4213

Go to **www.annualcreditreport.com** and you can receive your free credit reports on line or they can be printed.

Chapter 12

In Summary

We have touched on many subject areas dealing with Medical Insurance problems and the insurance industry as a whole. It is my sincere hope, that this book will give you guidance in your future dealings with the insurance industry and billing.

I also hope you enjoyed reading the personal and professional stories I have added to this book. I feel the book is helpful in many ways. It shows how hard the Medical Provider's staff does work to get your bill paid.

It also shows the different ways a small and a large billing office work. A large billing office sometimes does not go the extra miles to get your bill paid. It is just as easy to send you, the patient, to a Collection Agency.

Not all claims are denied the first time they are transmitted or mailed to the medical insurance companies. It is only a small percentage that is denied. This small percentage is what can amount to hours of trying to appease the insurance company and collecting your money.

If you have any questions, please contact me. Let me hear some of your horror stories. Every patient has them. I know I worked on many hard claims. I know the amount of work and stress you can put yourself through in order to get your claim paid. If you need professional help for a small fee I can help you.

Communicating with your Medical Insurance Company and your Medical Providers Offices is extremely stressful. It can cause your blood pressure to rise and, some say, steam to come out of your ears.

I hope you also now understand just how important knowing how the insurance terminology is when speaking to Medical Providers and your medical insurance company.

www.lindamecklerauthor.com
or email
lindamecklerauthor@yahoo.com

Disclaimer
Please keep in mind that I do not have all the answers to all of your problems and also, to not being a lawyer I do not know the legal positions of all I have shared with you. To know more, from the legal point of view, please consult your attorney.

Good Luck!

Linda Meckler

Published Book

by

Linda Meckler

Ghost Kids Trilogy

3 in one, book.

#1 - Ghost Kids

#2 - Blue Vase Mystery

#3 - Pirates' Treasure – The Hunt

Christy (12) and her brother Brad (16) meet two Ghost Kids in their new home. Uncle Charlie, the villain of the book, pops up in a magical Blue Vase. Adventures and mystery follow, ending with the Hunt for Pirates' Treasure. Family Values. Ages 8-14 to adult. 139 pages.

E Books available: on my website:

www.lindamecklerauthor.com

Boost Your Self-Esteem and Blossom

This is a collection of articles on family life and how to become a better family unit.

Computer Stations That Work

This book demonstrates how to set up a more ergonomic workstation either at home or at the office.

TTY Communication Book

This is a book on the subject of electronic equipment, the purpose of which is to help the deaf and mute to communicate. All the assistive technology communication equipment available is listed in this book.

Sleep Apnea With CPAP Machine

This is a book explaining step by step what to do when you think you have Sleep Apnea. It will take you through your doctor's visit, sleep study and end with the CPAP Machine.

Made in the USA
Monee, IL
04 November 2026

67377472R00075